Digging Up the Dead

FAMOUS GRAVEYARDS

By Kristen Rajczak

Gareth Stevens
PUBLISHING

Please visit our website, www.garethstevens.com. For a free color catalog of all our high-quality books, call toll free 1-800-542-2595 or fax 1-877-542-2596.

Library of Congress Cataloging-in-Publication Data

Rajczak, Kristen.
Famous graveyards / by Kristen Rajczak.
p. cm. – (Digging up the dead)
Includes index.
ISBN 978-1-4824-1269-7 (pbk.)
ISBN 978-1-4824-1232-1 (6-pack)
ISBN 978-1-4824-1486-8 (library binding)
1. Cemeteries – Juvenile literature. 2. Death – Social aspects – Juvenile literature. I.
Rajczak, Kristen. II. Title.
GT3320.R35 2015
363.7–d23

First Edition

Published in 2015 by
Gareth Stevens Publishing
111 East 14th Street, Suite 349
New York, NY 10003

Copyright © 2015 Gareth Stevens Publishing

Designer: Andrea Davison-Bartolotta
Editor: Greg Roza

Photo credits: Cover, p. 1 John Wang/Photographer's Choice RF/Getty Images;
cover, back cover, pp. 1–32 (background dirt texture) Kues/Shutterstock.com;
pp. 4, 7, 8, 10, 13, 14, 16, 18, 21, 22, 24, 27, 28 (gravestone) jayfish/
Shutterstock.com; p. 4 Raul Touzon/National Geographic/Getty Images; p. 5
Elzbieta Sekowska/Shutterstock.com; p. 7 JNS/Gamma-Rapho via Getty Images;
p. 8 Gavin Quirke/Lonely Planet Images/Getty Images; p. 9 Bildagentur Zoonar
GmbH/Shutterstock.com; pp. 10–11 Zvonimir Atletic/Shutterstock.com; p. 11 (inset)
Maksym Bondarchuk/Shutterstock.com; pp. 12–13 iolya/Shutterstock.com; p. 15
(main) © iStockphoto.com/JoffreyM; p. 15 (inset) Kim Traynor/Wikimedia Commons;
p. 17 Diana Mayfield/Lonely Planet Images/Getty Images; p. 17 (inset) Bertl123/
Shutterstock.com; p. 19 (main) Jess Kraft/Shutterstock.com; p. 19 (inset) Yu Lan/
Shutterstock.com; p. 21 (top) STR/AFP/Getty Images; p. 21 (bottom) MyLoupe/UIG via
Getty Images; p. 23 (main) Nagel Photography/Shutterstock.com; p. 23 (inset) Danita
Delimont/Gallo Images/Getty Images; p. 25 Aimin Tang/E+/Getty Images; p. 27
David Livingston/Getty Images; p. 29 (main) Saud A Faisal/Flickr/Getty Images; p. 29
(inset) Bertrand Guay/AFP/Getty Images.

Printed in the United States of America

CPSIA compliance information: Batch #CS15GS: For further information contact Gareth Stevens, New York, New York at 1-800-542-2595.

CONTENTS

Words in the glossary appear in **bold** type
the first time they are used in the text.

BURY THE DEAD

Graveyards exist to contain the dead. This means holding dead bodies as well as keeping death away from the living. Some people find the thought of death and dead bodies creepy and uncomfortable. However, some **cultures** celebrate the dead by visiting graveyards!

During the Mexican Day of the Dead, families visit cemeteries and decorate the graves of their loved ones. They welcome the spirits of the dead into their homes. The Japanese festival of Obon is sometimes called the Festival of Lanterns. Families light lanterns at homes and family graves to invite the dead back into the land of the living. Whether used to celebrate or simply house the dead, graveyards are found in every country around the world.

GRAVE MATTERS

Both cemeteries and graveyards are burial grounds. In the past, "graveyard" was used to mean a burial ground next to a church. Today, the words are used interchangeably.

Mexican cemetery decorated for Day of the Dead

A Family Affair

In most cultures, it has been the family's job to take care of their dead. Family **mausoleums** and grave plots are common in the United States and around the world. People want to stay close to their family even after death. The location of graves is often carefully chosen. In China, it may be based on feng shui (FUHNG SHWEE), which is a way of arranging something so it has the most favorable flow of energy.

The look of a graveyard largely depends on where and when it was built. Shown here is a Buddhist cemetery in Thailand.

OLD JEWISH CEMETERY

How could thousands of graves fit in just one city block? By building up! Prague, Czech Republic, was home to some of the wealthiest Jewish citizens in Europe. However, city laws didn't allow them to bury their dead anywhere except one particular city block. So, as the block filled up, more earth was brought and placed over the existing graves. This began during the 15th century and continued until 1787.

It's believed there are many layers of earth and graves buried on top of each other. About 12,000 tombstones can be seen at the top of the graveyard. In 1891, the New Jewish Cemetery was built to replace the older cemetery. It's the only Jewish cemetery in Prague today.

Separate Cemeteries

For centuries, Jews were **persecuted** throughout Europe. Few Jewish gravestones have been found from the early **Middle Ages**, which probably means they weren't living in big communities. Starting around the 11th century, Jews were forced into separate cemeteries by Christians who were burying their dead in and around their churches. Jewish cemeteries were set up on the outskirts of towns and were often surrounded by walls. This continued for hundreds of years, making overcrowding in Jewish cemeteries a problem all over Europe, not just in Prague.

The gravestones at the Old Jewish Cemetery are very close together, showing just how little space the Jewish community had to bury their dead—even after building up their cemetery!

GRAVE MATTERS

Some groups, including Jews, worried about whether cemeteries spread illnesses. Many cemeteries were established outside city walls because of this fear.

CITY OF THE DEAD

Imagine sleeping in one room with all the members of your family—including some who've already died. That's what thousands of people do every day in an Islamic cemetery in Cairo, Egypt. Known as the City of the Dead, the cemetery was first used during the 7th century. It's about 4 miles (6.4 km) long now and includes around 1 million tombs, or walled buildings housing graves. It's inside these rooms that the poor of Cairo have made their homes.

Egyptians have long believed that cemeteries are part of a community. Those living in the City of the Dead have surely taken this to heart, and visitors say the residents are welcoming and kind. No one knows exactly how many people live there among the dead.

GRAVE MATTERS

The City of the Dead is also called el-Arafa necropolis. *Necro-* means "having to do with death or dead bodies," and *-opolis* means "city."

Just Making Room

Cairo is one of the most populous cities in the world. However, there isn't enough housing for everyone who lives there. This is one of the major reasons the poor of the city have moved into the tombs of the City of the Dead. In fact, some families have been living there for hundreds of years. Living in the cemetery is illegal, but officials aren't enforcing the laws about it.

The people living in the City of the Dead may use gravestones as tables or desks. They hang their laundry on lines strung between the tombs.

PÈRE LACHAISE

In 1804, the French emperor Napoleon established Père Lachaise (PEHR lah-SHEZ), a cemetery in which he said "every citizen has the right to be buried regardless of race or religion." Found in northeastern Paris, France, Père Lachaise has about 300,000 graves, surrounded by well-kept, winding paths with their own names.

Père Lachaise is more often known as a beautiful place to visit than a spooky graveyard. It's one of the most visited cemeteries in the world, with hundreds of thousands of people coming each year. The elaborate monuments around the cemetery are just part of the draw. Many historic people are buried there, including author Gertrude Stein, singer Maria Callas, and composer Frederic Chopin. The tomb of writer Oscar Wilde is often covered with red lipstick kisses!

GRAVE MATTERS

Tens of thousands of French Jews who died in **concentration camps** during World War II are honored by memorials within Père Lachaise.

Jim Morrison

Singer for the band the Doors, Jim Morrison, is buried in Père Lachaise. Marked by a rather small, black granite stone, his grave used to have a statue of Morrison's head on it, but that was stolen. In 1991, a riot occurred in the cemetery when thousands flocked to Morrison's grave for the 20th anniversary of his death. Today, the stone is guarded from the huge crowds that still come to pay their respects to the rock legend.

Trees line the walkways through Père Lachaise, and moss grows on many of the monuments.

HIGHGATE CEMETERY

Established in 1839, Highgate Cemetery near London, England, would be a beautiful place to be laid to rest—if it weren't haunted! Highgate is known for the lovely trees and flowers that grow naturally among the graves—as well as several spooky happenings. Glowing red eyes, the ghost of an old insane woman, and other creepy sightings are among the tales told about Highgate Cemetery. The story about the Highgate **vampire** attacking visitors might be the most frightening.

More famous still are some of those buried in Highgate Cemetery. **Philosopher** Karl Marx might be the biggest name, though author of *The Hitchhiker's Guide to the Galaxy* Douglas Adams is buried there, as is another famous writer—George Eliot.

It's Cramped in Here!

As early as the 6th century, European cemeteries were crowded. Coffins were buried on top of each other. Old bones were dug up to make room for the more recently dead. By the 1800s in London, people were buried in graveyards just about everywhere—and they weren't cared for well. Many were concerned about the public health problems this could cause. From 1833 to 1841, seven cemeteries were founded in the English countryside near London to create more burial space. Highgate was one of these.

Highgate Cemetery was part of the English government's efforts to better the burial practices in populous London. Today, there are more than 170,000 people buried there.

GRAVE MATTERS

Until about the 19th century in Europe, some people weren't allowed to be buried in cemeteries, including murderers and those who were thought to be witches.

13

GREYFRIARS KIRKYARD

Would you visit a graveyard considered one of the most haunted in the world? Greyfriars Kirkyard in Edinburgh, Scotland, has millions of tourists a year—and some leave marked by the visit. Connected to the kirkyard, or churchyard, is Covenanters' Prison, a place where 1,200 revolutionaries were jailed in the late 1600s. Many were hanged or forced into slavery. Only 257 of them lived to tell about the horrible treatment they received in the prison. Touring the empty prison today, people report being scratched, burned, bruised, and worse by the ghosts inside.

The lawyer who imprisoned the Covenanters, "bloody" George MacKenzie, was buried in Greyfriars in 1691. Stories say that in 1999, someone opened his grave, the Black Mausoleum, and let his spirit out. The spirit is **aggressive**—and some say even murderous!

GRAVE MATTERS

Fans of the Harry Potter book series leave notes on a 197-year-old grave in the kirkyard. The gravestone reads "Thomas Riddell," a close match for Tom Riddle, the real name of the series' cruel and powerful villain wizard.

Mary Queen of Scots established the kirkyard in 1562. In 1587, Mary was executed for trying to have the then-ruler of Britain, Elizabeth I, killed. Mary was beheaded.

Body Snatchers!

Digging up the dead has gone on for centuries, but at Greyfriars Kirkyard it wasn't to make room for new graves. Bodies were dug up and sold to medical students at the University of Edinburgh during the early 1800s. The consequences of this body-snatching trade can still be seen today. Some graves have iron bars over them, called mortsafes. Families put them in to keep their loved ones' graves from being disturbed.

mortsafe

ZENTRALFRIEDHOF

Found outside Vienna, Austria, Zentralfriedhof (tsehn-TRAHL-freed-hof)—the Vienna Central Cemetery—is Europe's second-largest cemetery in area at about 618 acres (250 ha). It's the largest graveyard in Europe by the number of people buried there, with about 3 million.

In the center of Zentralfriedhof stands the Cemetery Church of St. Charles Borromeo. A dome 192 feet (58.5 m) tall tops the church, which opened in 1911. During World War II, a bomb seriously damaged both the dome and the roof. About 12,000 graves and numerous **crypts** were destroyed as well. The church was eventually restored. Visitors can explore covered footpaths on either side of the church that contain 768 columbaria **niches**. These are spaces in the wall that hold coffins or **cremated** remains.

GRAVE MATTERS

Since it opened in 1874, Zentralfriedhof has accepted the remains of followers of all religions. There are individual sections for each religion, in addition to a part for people who donated their bodies to science.

Honorary Graves

The remains of many famous people were moved to Zentralfriedhof's section for honorary graves. In order to be eligible for an honorary grave there, a person must have made a contribution to music, art, writing, or science, or be a politician who helped Austria in some way. There are about 1,000 honorary graves in Zentralfriedhof. Composers Beethoven, Brahms, and Schubert are just a few who are buried there.

LA RECOLETA

La Recoleta Cemetery in Buenos Aires, Argentina, is a public cemetery. However, it's filled with the remains of some of the most powerful and wealthy Argentine citizens in recent history. Presidents, generals, and governors are laid to rest here. So many, in fact, that there aren't any more tombs for sale! The only remains **interred** today are those belonging to families that already own mausoleums in La Recoleta.

The social class of those buried in La Recoleta is obvious from the beautifully adorned mausoleums and graves. You might mistake it for an outdoor art gallery! A number of the mausoleums are considered national historic monuments. Some include statues of angels and saints. Others bear engravings and other decorations. The resting places of military remains are often watched over by stone soldiers.

GRAVE MATTERS

The mausoleums in La Recoleta have family names on them. Each family member's name is engraved on a plaque with their death date—but not usually their birth date—and fixed to the mausoleum.

All the mausoleums in La Recoleta are aboveground. The cemetery is laid out like a city, with tree-lined main walkways. Sidewalks that branch from the main walkways are lined with mausoleums.

Following the Remains of Eva Perón

The most visited gravesite in La Recoleta is that of former Argentine First Lady Eva Perón. However, her body wasn't interred there until 24 years after her death. Three years after she died in 1952, her husband, Juan Perón, was overthrown. Eva's body was taken from Buenos Aires and buried in Italy under a false name. In 1971, it was moved to Juan Perón's home in Spain, where it stayed until 1974. In 1976, Eva Perón was moved to her family mausoleum in La Recoleta.

19

BABAOSHAN REVOLUTIONARY CEMETERY

The Babaoshan Revolutionary Cemetery in Beijing, China, is directly tied to the rise of the **communist** government in the country. When the People's Republic of China was founded in 1949, the creation of a cemetery especially for those who died fighting for its establishment was ordered. The Babaoshan Revolutionary Cemetery opened in 1951. Today, being interred in Babaoshan is a great honor reserved for high-ranking military and political leaders, as well as scientists and writers.

Cremated remains are kept in niches made in long walls. Where a person's niche is in the cemetery tells how powerful or well known they were. The cemetery's graves and tombs are also sized and placed depending on a person's rank in society.

A Wait for Burial

As of October 2013, families wanting a niche for their dead in Babaoshan were told they would have to wait until June 2014, when space for 10,000 more niches would be complete. There isn't any more room for graves. Babaoshan isn't alone. The city of Hong Kong, China, has dealt with overcrowded cemeteries for years. They've built many-story buildings for the dead, and recently a graveyard ship that would float on the South China Sea was proposed!

The Babaoshan expansion will include another wall of niches. Since there are a limited number available, each will cost about $19,000!

hanging coffins of
Shennong Stream, China

GRAVE MATTERS

While not exactly a graveyard, hanging coffins are found at several locations in China. Two coffins hanging in the Wuyi Mountains are about 3,000 years old!

GETTYSBURG NATIONAL CEMETERY

In 1863, during the American Civil War, thousands of soldiers died at the Battle of Gettysburg. Burying them would have been a huge task, and one the Union Army didn't have time for. Citizens from the nearby town of Gettysburg, Pennsylvania, were brought in to help. The bodies weren't identified, preserved, or buried in any organized way. The bodies had already started to smell and draw flies, so the goal was to do the job quickly.

A national cemetery for the Union dead—today's Gettysburg National Cemetery—was established near the battlefield site just a few months later. The bodies had to be disinterred, or dug up, and reburied. About 100 bodies a day arrived at the new cemetery. When President Abraham Lincoln gave his famous Gettysburg Address there, the reburying hadn't been finished yet.

GRAVE MATTERS

Particularly in times of great **casualties**, such as war, mass graves may be used to bury the dead. During the Battle of Gettysburg, there were so many dead that soldiers, especially Confederates, were interred together in mass graves near where they died.

The Gettysburg National Cemetery is home to the graves of many war veterans, such as those who fought in the Spanish American War, World War I, World War II, the Korean War, and the Vietnam War.

Military Cemeteries

The total number of deaths in the Civil War is estimated at about 620,000. That's about twice the number of Americans who died in World War II. Burying the huge number of dead became a major concern. As a result, Congress created the national cemetery system in 1862. Today, there are 200 military cemeteries for veterans, casualties of war, and their families. This includes 24 located outside the United States.

ARLINGTON NATIONAL CEMETERY

Arlington was another cemetery created during the American Civil War. The land in Virginia was home to the Confederate general Robert E. Lee until the Union army took it over in 1861. It became a national cemetery in 1864.

More than 400,000 American soldiers and veterans are buried in Arlington National Cemetery. Many historic figures are buried there, too, including President William Howard Taft and President John F. Kennedy. A special request from the city of Washington, DC, brought the remains of Pierre Charles L'Enfant to Arlington in 1909. L'Enfant was the Frenchman who planned Washington, DC. After his death in 1825, he was buried in Green Hill, Maryland. In 1909, L'Enfant was disinterred and moved to Arlington. In 1911, a monument over the new gravesite was dedicated to him.

GRAVE MATTERS

Plantations in the American South were often too far from churches for family members to be buried in church graveyards. Family cemeteries were built on the plantation, often on high ground and surrounded by a fence or wall.

Robert E. Lee's wife's family owned Arlington House, the mansion that still stands in Arlington National Cemetery, though he also lived there. Her parents are still buried in their original graves on the grounds.

Rural Cemeteries

Have you ever spent the afternoon in a beautifully laid out cemetery? Americans began building parklike cemeteries during the 1830s. There weren't public parks and gardens to play in, so people used cemeteries for picnics, hunting, and carriage races. Flowers and trees, rolling hills, and decorative gravestones invited people to enjoy nature, not just visit the dead. Cemeteries were to be totally enclosed "to give them an air of security and seclusion…a suitable resting place and home for the dead."

eternal flame honoring
President John F. Kennedy

HOLLYWOOD CEMETERIES

The Forest Lawn Memorial Parks in Glendale and the Hollywood Hills, California, are two of the most star-studded graveyards in the world. The Glendale cemetery includes the gravesites of Michael Jackson, L. Frank Baum (author of *The Wizard of Oz*), and Walt Disney. However, finding your favorite star's headstone can be a challenge. Glendale has more than 250,000 graves! Employees of the cemetery don't like helping visitors find a certain grave.

The Hollywood Forever Cemetery in Hollywood, California, might be an easier bet if you want to see a celebrity's grave. Punk rock star Johnny Ramone, movie director Cecil B. DeMille, and many movie stars from the mid-1900s are buried there—and the cemetery's website will show you exactly where!

Headstone Style

Memorial parks like Forest Lawn look a bit different from some of the very old graveyards mentioned in this book. That's partly because the main style of headstone has changed over time. In the 1800s, angels, sleeping children, and other decorative carvings adorned gravestones. By the 1900s, flat stones or simple crosses with the name and dates of birth and death were more common. Today, some grave markers point up as a reminder of hope.

Forest Lawn Memorial Park, Glendale, Celebrity Graves

name	died	famous for
Humphrey Bogart	1957	acting in many movies, including *Casablanca*
Nat King Cole	1965	singing "The Christmas Song"; first black performer to host a variety TV show
Sam Cooke	1964	soul and pop music, including "A Change Is Gonna Come"
Dorothy Dandridge	1965	first black woman to be nominated for an Academy Award
Sammy Davis Jr.	1990	actor and singer in the Rat Pack with Frank Sinatra and Dean Martin
Errol Flynn	1955	acting in many movies, including *The Charge of the Light Brigade* and *Robin Hood*
Jean Harlow	1937	acting in many movies, including *Dinner at Eight*
Mary Pickford	1979	acting in silent films; founding United Artists
Elizabeth Taylor	2011	acting in many movies, including *Cleopatra*

Fans have certainly found Michael Jackson's grave! There are often flowers and pictures on it.

GRAVE MATTERS

A memorial park is a type of cemetery, but it's even more parklike since the grave markers are flat and understated.

WHY VISIT?

Graveyards are some of the biggest tourist attractions in big cities around the world. People will travel from far away to visit some famed graves. From thrill seekers looking for the haunted chills of the Greyfriars Kirkyard to art lovers admiring La Recoleta, they have many different reasons for doing so. But perhaps the lessons graveyard visitors can learn are what keep people coming back.

Graveyards reflect a culture's ideas about death. Those who are grieving the death of a veteran might find a feeling of community among the plain, white crosses in Arlington National Cemetery. Or those searching for the meaning of death could see beautiful mausoleums and understand how it could be celebrated. Then again, tourists might just want to pay their respects to the remains of their favorite celebrity.

GRAVE MATTERS

If you find yourself in a famous graveyard, read the headstones around you. You can learn a lot about a person's life by what kind of grave marker they have and the facts on it, like their birth date.

Pet Cemeteries

Just outside Paris is Le Cimetière des Chiens—the dog cemetery. It was the first pet cemetery in the world when it opened in 1899. Many upper-class people had large graves and statues made for their beloved pets. Many of the graves are for dogs, but many others are for cats, birds, horses, and even a monkey. One famous dog is buried there. The grave of Rin Tin Tin, who was in movies in the 1920s, often has flowers on it.

29

GLOSSARY

aggressive: showing a readiness to attack

casualty: someone who dies during war

communist: someone who practices communism, which is a government system in which the government controls what is used to make and transport products, and there is no privately owned property

concentration camp: a camp where political prisoners are imprisoned

cremate: to burn to ashes

crypt: a chamber, partly or completely underground, where people are buried

culture: the customs, arts, social institutions, and achievements of a particular nation or group of people

inter: to put a dead body in a grave or tomb

mausoleum: a large tomb aboveground that may also be a monument

Middle Ages: a time in European history from about AD 500 to AD 1500

niche: a hollow place in a wall that can hold a small object

persecuted: being treated in a harmful way for being different

philosopher: thinker

vampire: a made-up being believed to be a dead person who comes back to life and drinks human blood

FOR MORE INFORMATION

Books

Burrows, Jennifer. *Arlington National Cemetery.* Vero Beach, FL: Rourke, 2010.

Everett, J. H., and Marilyn Scott-Waters. *Haunted Histories: Creepy Castles, Dark Dungeons, and Powerful Palaces.* New York, NY: Holt and Company, 2012.

Lynette, Rachel. *Burial Grounds.* Detroit, MI: KidHaven Press, 2009.

Websites

Arlington National Cemetery Facts
www.washingtondc-go.com/attractions/arlington-national-cemetery-facts.html
Learn more about this famous US cemetery.

Top 10 Cemeteries to Visit
travel.nationalgeographic.com/travel/top-10/cemeteries/#page=1
Find out about more famous cemeteries in National Geographic's list of the top cemeteries to visit around the world.

INDEX